FOXES

First published in Great Britain in 2000 by
Colin Baxter Photography Ltd
Grantown-on-Spey
Moray PH26 3NA
Scotland

Text © David Macdonald 2000

WorldLife Library Series

A CIP Catalogue record for this book is available from the British Library.

ISBN 1-84107-041-6

Photographs © 2000:

Front cover © Laurie Campbell
Back cover © Niall Benvie (BBC Natural History Unit)
Page 1 © Kennan Ward
Page 3 © David Macdonald
Page 4 © Andy Rouse (NHPA)
Page 6 © Kennan Ward
Page 9 © Arthur Morris (Windrush Photos)
Page 11 © Robert Franz (Planet Earth Pictures)
Page 12 © Marilyn Kazmers (Still Pictures)
Page 15 © Rod Williams (Planet Earth Pictures)
Page 16 © Nigel J Dennis (NHPA)
Page 19 © Heather Angel
Page 20 © Michael Evan Sewell
Page 23 © S Cordier (Auscape)
Page 24 © Harry M Walker
Page 27a © Ashod Francis Papazian (NHPA)
Page 27b © Paul Van Gaalen (Bruce Coleman)
Page 27c © Steven C Kaufman (Bruce Coleman)
Page 28 © Laurie Campbell
Page 31 © Laurie Campbell

Page 32 © Norbert Rosing
Page 35 © Heather Angel
Page 37 © Harry M Walker
Page 38 © Kim Taylor (Bruce Coleman)
Page 41 © Stephen J Krasemann (Bruce Coleman)
Page 42 © Arthur Morris (Windrush Photos)
Page 45 © Karen Ward (Kennan Ward)
Page 47 © Rod Williams (Bruce Coleman)
Page 48 © Mark Hamblin (Woodfall Wild Images)
Page 51 © B Brochier (Still Pictures)
Page 53 © Tom Schandy (Bruce Coleman)
Page 54 © Mark Hamblin (Woodfall Wild Images)
Page 57 © Norbert Rosing
Page 58 © William S Paton (Bruce Coleman)
Page 60 © Colin Varndell (Bruce Coleman)
Page 61 © Colin Varndell (Bruce Coleman)
Page 62 © Mark Hamblin (Woodfall Wild Images)
Page 65 © David Tomlinson (Windrush Photos)
Page 66 © Staffan Widstrand (Bruce Coleman)
Page 69 © Kennan Ward

Printed in China

FOXES

David Macdonald

Colin Baxter Photography, Grantown-on-Spey, Scotland

Contents

Introduction

The ominous shadow of the earth had just slipped across a round-faced moon on 4 April 1996 when the first of three orphan fox cubs began to suck. We named her Eclipse, and her sisters, Moonshine and Comet. Three blind, snub-nosed, mewling, mahogany-colored cubs whose warmly acrid smell is re-awakened in my nose as I write these words. These were, I reckon, somewhere between the thirtieth and fortieth red fox cubs I had hand-reared. Now, the task was made easier because my children, Ewan, Fiona and Isobel, were allocated one cub each on which to dote throughout the Easter school holidays.

The arrival of the cubs brought flooding back memories of Niff, the first vulpine adoptee to survive my ministrations almost a quarter of a century before, and back further to the moment, pushing 40 years ago, when my first accolade at school was won with plaster casts of fox footprints, reverentially sculpted from the sand of a golf-course bunker. In the meantime, aside from radio tracking more than 200 red foxes in places as distant as Oxfordshire and Saudi Arabia (and as diverse as mountain top and factory floor), I have been led around the world by their cousins. I've studied Arctic foxes in the tundra, crab-eating foxes in Amazonia, swift foxes in the Canadian prairies, kit foxes in Mexico's Chihuahuan desert, Rüppell's foxes in Arabia and the fairy-footed Blanford's foxes of Israel, not to mention their canid kin such as coyotes, bush dogs, jackals of all three kinds and Ethiopian wolves with which I have also been enmeshed. But why? Why has it seemed like a good idea to devote so much of a lifetime to trying to get inside the skin of these creatures?

Red foxes are now the most widespread of the wild dog family, the Canidae. The stunning adaptability that leads them to hold this record, and to thrive under radically contrasting extremes of climate and habitat, also brings them into diverse conflicts with people. The problems range from the large and life-threatening, like rabies, through to more local, but no less hotly debated, such as the loss of livestock. When the boy besotted with animals had to become a man with a profession, it struck me that it was not merely interesting, but also potentially useful

A red fox cub, at about two months old.

to try and understand red foxes better. Furthermore, their relatives are similarly enthralling – of those I have been involved with, Ethiopian wolves are the rarest on earth, coyotes among the most loathed, bush dogs the least known and African wild dogs perhaps the most controversial. These are all reasons why it is worthwhile to understand better this intriguing group of mammals.

Of course, there are other reasons why foxes in particular, and canids in general, are interesting, and one is their close relationship with domestic dogs. The evolutionary history of the dog family causes it to be split between two principal branches, the lupine or wolf-like canids and the vulpine or fox-like ones. The domestic dog was domesticated from the wolf, an event dated by archaeologists at 14,000 years ago, but, controversially, more recent molecular studies push this back to 135,000 years ago. Foxes may have separated from the lupine line five to seven million years ago, but they are still beguilingly similar to the wolf at the fireside in their behavior. Anybody who has an eye for domestic dog behavior, and can read their body language, can immediately recognize the same traits in foxes and – I can assure you – foxes have at least the same depth of individuality that captivates any dog-owner. Indeed, I suspect that it is this blend of familiar dogness with untamedness that provokes such a deep wrath tinged with respect in many rural people regarding the perceived predatory misdemeanors of red foxes. Yet, foxes are not domesticated, indeed, having mentioned Eclipse and her sisters, I should explain that the foxes I have hand-reared are more appropriately thought of as professional colleagues than as pets: I have worked with them closely to understand their wildness, not to bend them to domesticity. Hand-rearing foxes is not something that most people are equipped to undertake, and for those that attempt it – however well-intentioned they might be – the result is generally sadness.

Of course, another appeal of foxes is the challenge they pose to fieldcraft. They are so finely honed to avoid human attention that there is a terrific thrill in stalking close enough to probe their secrets. I was fortunate to begin my research at a time when the first night-vision scopes became available to biologists, a marvelous tool that lifts the veil of the darkest night. For example, I remember the night when I was able to watch an old vixen, Toothypeg, as she taught her young cub the intricacies of catching earthworms on one of his first foraging trips away from the den. At night, earthworms poke their heads above ground, their tails anchored in the soil, and adult foxes deftly grasp them in their front teeth and draw them from their burrows. On that night,

A red fox, photographed in Utah, U.S.A. – the same species occurs in both North America and Europe, and across Eurasia. This gives the red fox, which has also been introduced to Australia, the widest geographical range of any wild member of the dog family.

when I first saw Toothypeg's cub, he was pouncing fruitlessly on these slithery prey. However, as her cub watched, Toothypeg began to catch worms, but instead of pulling them clear from their burrow, she held them taut, while her frolicking offspring clumsily attempted to pull them free. At the first two attempts he fumbled, but his attention was caught and he had abandoned his initial pouncing attacks (good for catching mice but completely useless for a slippery earthworm). Astonished, I watched for ten long seconds as Toothypeg gently tapped with her forepaw to persuade an obstinate earthworm to relax its anchorage on its burrow, until it was two-thirds drawn from the ground. Then she held it still for the cub to snatch greedily. As I continued to watch, the transformation was clear: the cub, on his own, was still inept at catching earthworms, but he had grasped his mother's technique. When I next stalked close to him, almost a month later, he was drawing earthworms from their burrows like an old pro!

The future of the world's three dozen or so species of wild canids shares the gloomy uncertainties that threaten all of Nature. The root cause is the reckless growth of the planet's human population, but more immediately, wild canids have their own problems. For those which travel prodigiously expansive ranges, the loss and fragmentation of habitats confines them in perilously small numbers to slivers of wilderness. Even protected areas have borders, beyond which straying predators often encounter an outside world bristling with human hostility: it is an unhappy fact of geometry that smaller refuges have disproportionately more border to inner sanctuary. Being opportunists, wild canids sometimes kill domestic stock and attract the understandably murderous (but often fruitless) revenge of the bereaved stockman. They are also blighted by having valuable pelts, by making entertaining quarry (a pastime facilitated by the seemingly universal loathing with which domestic dogs regard their wild relatives), and by being prone to a perplexing array of infectious diseases (many now transmitted by domestic dogs, which also pose, to their closer wild cousins, a threat of hybridization). But against these tribulations, canids include some remarkable post-modern survivors. Above all, the red fox, triumphant from tundra to concrete jungle, and arguably the most beautiful of them all, carries into the second millennium the banner of the world's most successful wild dog.

The Arctic fox occurs in two colour morphs, of which one is pure white in winter.

Origins

Foxes, along with wolves, jackals and their kind, belong to the Canidae, the dog family. The canids are carnivores – they not only live a carnivorous life but also belong to the order Carnivora. All members of the Carnivora have one characteristic in common: they, (or their ancestors), possess carnassial teeth (scissor teeth – for shearing through flesh).

The first members of the dog family, the dawn dogs, *Hesperocyon*, hunted the canopy of the jungle that cloaked the northern hemisphere 35 million years ago. Dawn dogs had long tails and low-slung bodies which doubtless slipped easily beneath the forest undergrowth. Meanwhile their cat-like contemporary, the sabre-toothed *Hoplophoneus*, wrestled prey to the ground and delivered a stabbing bite. Although the dawn dogs had scissor-teeth, these were blunter, and were backed by broad, spiky-cusped molar teeth designed to crunch as well as cut. So while *Hoplophoneus* filleted its feast with carnassials that sliced easily through flesh, *Hesperocyon* chewed beetles, small mammals, eggs, grubs and fruit.

About five to seven million years ago, some dogs moved north to the Bering land-bridge joining North America to Asia and, hence, Europe. Either just before or just after they crossed, an early dog called *Canis davisii* gave rise to the two main lineages found today: the fox-like vulpine dogs and the wolf-like lupine dogs. Before this split the early dogs gave rise to the ancestors of today's Far Eastern raccoon dog, *Nyctereutes procyonoides* and North America's gray foxes, *Urocyon cinereoargenteus*.

The arrival of dogs in Eurasia coincided with the demise of most of their rivals. Around this time the last of the Creodonts (the dominant meat-eaters of the period) died out along with the amphicyonids (the half-dogs, or bear-dogs, members of the one now extinct Carnivore family) and most of the hyenas which had until then occupied what was then to become the dog's niche. The canids cannot be blamed for these extinctions, which were probably precipitated by the changing climate. However, they meant that the dogs arrived in the right place at the right time, to fill niches left vacant by the demise of potential rivals.

The first offshoot of the lupine dogs in the Old World were the ancestors of the modern bat-eared fox, *Otocyon megalotis*, of Africa. The earliest vulpine lineage to split off led to the

Cape fox, *Vulpes chama*, which is now the only vulpine species found south of the Sahara. Another vulpine lineage led to the red fox, *V. vulpes*, which soon spanned Eurasia and early on gave rise to the plains-dwelling Corsac fox, *V. corsac*, of the Russian steppes. With the frozen Bering crossing behind it, the red fox lineage trekked south to sun and sand, adapting to circumstances no less harsh, and giving rise to the ancestors of the arid-land swift fox, *V. velox*, and Rüppell's fox, *V. ruppelli*. About three to four million years ago a fox-like ancestor, perhaps an offshoot of the Cape fox line, found itself facing the climatic changes that produced the first deserts in the Middle East and northern Africa. It produced two desert specialists: the fennec, *F. zerda*, and Blanford's fox, *V. cana*.

While the foxes were radiating into a diversity of species, the lupine lineage was also proving remarkably successful. An ancestor named *C. arnensis* probably gave rise to early progenitors of both the modern coyote, *C. latrans*, and the gray wolf, *C. lupus*. Both flourished in Europe during the Pleistocene (one to two million years ago). The coyote (no longer found in the Old World but now remarkably successful in North America and particularly well-adapted to life alongside man and agriculture) crossed back to North America two million years ago, along with various foxes and pantherine cats. One school of thought believes that the gray wolf crossed to America a little later than the coyote (approximately 700,000 years ago); an alternative view is that the gray wolf descends from a canid that had never left America. The end result was that wolves became the most widespread wild mammal in the world, spanning Europe, Asia and America. The same lupine stock that produced the wolf and coyote also produced two closely related jackals, the golden, *C. aureus*, and side-striped, *C. adustus*. In contrast, an earlier lupine lineage produced the black-backed jackal, *C. mesomelas*, and such pack hunters as the dhole, *Cuon alpinus*, which ranges from Siberia to south-east Asia, and the African wild dog, *Lycaon pictus*, whose ancestors crossed to Africa five million years ago.

The pack hunters of the plains, in more recent times, have suffered severely at the hands of humans. People destroyed the herds and habitat that supported them, and viewed all but the tiniest canids as competitors. While we coveted the domestic dog, we relentlessly exterminated its wild kin. In Europe, some large canids have been virtually annihilated.

The Corsac fox is a small Eurasian fox about which almost nothing is known in the wild.

Foxes of the World

Foxes are small canids with pointed muzzles, somewhat flattened slender skulls, large triangular ears and long bushy tails. They have lithe builds, long legs and four-toed feet, tipped with non-retractile claws (their feet are called digitigrade, which means they walk on their toes). Their two wrist bones (the scaphoid and the lunar) are fused and the front leg bones (radius and ulna) locked: both adaptations for running. Their entire body structure, along with various other adaptations, reflects their swift, enduring predatory lifestyle.

There are approximately 23 species of fox around the world, including the 13 vulpine foxes (genus *Vulpes*) of the northern hemisphere, the eight zorros of South America (distinct from the vulpine lineage, in fact, descended from the lupine lineage), the bat-eared fox, distinguished by its adaptations to an insectivorous lifestyle and the Arctic fox, distinguished by its skull characteristics and adaptations to a polar environment. Members of the genus *Vulpes* span North America and the north of South America, Europe, Africa and Asia.

The beautiful gray fox of the southern U.S.A. and Central America is the oldest surviving dog, having evolved six to nine million years ago, and lives today much like the dawn dogs once did. With dainty steps, territorial pairs move nimbly through deciduous woodland and deserted farmland, searching for insects, fruits, carrion and small mammals up to the size of rabbits. With a flamboyant fluffy tail, the gray fox is as delicate in appearance as in movement. Its long, brindled gray/black fur merges with pastel buffs and oranges on its neck, legs, flanks and cheeks, and its face and underside are patterned in white. By the standard of today's dogs, it is a good climber, being able to rotate its forelegs to clasp branches or rocks. In its distinctly three-dimensional world, hunting in cliff crevice, tree bowl and root hole, a gray fox in a hurry moves like a spring-loaded powder-puff.

The swift fox crossed back from Eurasia to North America little more than half a million years ago and adapted to the vast arid lands of the North American prairies. Unusually among canids, the swift fox, at 4 lb 6 oz–6 lb 9 oz (2–3 kg), sometimes hunts alone for prey

The Cape fox of the Kalahari desert is the southernmost vulpine.

larger than itself, pursuing jackrabbits at speeds that can top 30 mph (50 kmph). During cool periods of the Ice Age, rolling glaciers pushed south, converting the fox's prairie home to tundra. In response, some 250,000 years ago, the swift fox gave rise to the Arctic fox, *Alopex lagopus*.

The modern Arctic fox's range encircles the North Pole from Alaska to Kamchatka, like a skullcap on the globe. This astoundingly beautiful creature is a monument to the endurance of its kind. The 6 lb 8 oz–9 lb (3–4 kg) Arctic fox has relatively short ears, legs and tail to cut heat loss, and its paws are swathed in fluffy mittens of wooly fur. In terms of appearance it is the most distinct of the foxes. About 70 per cent of the Arctic fox's fur fiber is fine underfur, compared with 20 per cent in red foxes. Its fur is so luxuriant that the Arctic fox begins to shiver only when the temperature drops to –70°C (–94°F). Indeed, an Arctic fox caught in a run-of-the-mill blizzard is more likely to be troubled by heatstroke than frostbite.

Arctic foxes breed on the tundra from 53° N, level with the southern tip of Hudson Bay, to the snowy wastes north of Greenland at 88° N. As the tundra squeezes a whole year's growth into the two-month summer, the Arctic fox races to breed. It also has to contend with the boom or bust ecology of the far north. A four-year cycle in populations of its lemming and vole prey transforms the banqueting ground of one year to a field of famine in another. In Barrow, Alaska, brown lemmings may soar to over 494 per acre (200 per hectare) in one year, then plummet to less than three per acre (one per ha) in another. Arctic foxes disappear from Barrow during the troughs, but swarm in at 65 per sq mile (25 per sq km) during the peaks. They are able to take advantage of the booms by breeding more prolifically than any other canid. The Arctic fox is equipped with a record-breaking 12 to 16 teats, only rivaled by the African wild dog with 12 to 14. It can sustain litters which can average more than 11 cubs, the record being 19 in one litter.

Meanwhile, retreating from the ice, the swift foxes survived in warmer enclaves and eventually gave rise to another, but very similar, species: the kit fox, *V. macrotis*. Until recently, swift foxes were extinct in Canada (the last of the Canadian swift foxes was shot by European

Arctic foxes have a circumpolar distribution, but have been declining fast in Scandinavia.

*The San Joaquin kit fox of California is an endangered sub-species;
apart from habitat loss, its downfall has been interspecific aggression from
coyotes – in general, large canids tend to persecute their smaller cousins.*

settlers before 1938), and their future throughout the United States may be in jeopardy. Almost 80 per cent of the mixed grass biome has disappeared in Canada and the canid equation has changed from one where swift foxes and wolves dominated, to one where red foxes and coyotes are now prevalent. This is especially disheartening knowing that 65–85 per cent of swift-fox mortalities are coyote kills.

Kit foxes in Mexico fare somewhat better in a more productive landscape. During a study of swift foxes in Canada and kit foxes in Mexico, approximately 80 per cent of the swift foxes monitored in Canada died over an 800-day period (at least 40 per cent of these being due to coyotes – many others were killed by eagles). None of the monitored kit foxes in Mexico died over a similar length of time, despite living in the presence of a similar density of potentially threatening coyotes. The answer to this apparent puzzle may be explained by the habitat in which the swift and kit foxes live. Mexican kit foxes have home-range sizes approximately a quarter of the size of the swift fox in Canada – between 4 and 5½ sq miles (10 and 14 sq km) as opposed to 17 sq miles (43 sq km). Having less distance to travel to find food, Mexican kit foxes are likely to come into contact with coyotes less often than their Canadian counterparts. Furthermore, if a Mexican kit fox does come across a coyote there are ample fox-sized holes into which it may escape (26.7 holes/ha in prairie dog towns, 2.3 holes/ha in kangaroo-rat dominated grasslands). A Canadian swift fox encountering a coyote has to find a single bolthole in an average of 5 acres (2 ha). As a result of a major swift fox reintroduction project, approximately 300 individuals now occupy two sites in Canada. Of the individuals captured by biologists, 80 per cent are now wild-born and the project may be one of the most successful carnivore reintroductions ever undertaken.

Red foxes have the most expansive geographical distribution of all foxes, and indeed, of any wild carnivore. They are found throughout almost all of the northern hemisphere, as well as in Australia, as a result of human introductions. In North America they span the continent from the Aleutian Islands to Newfoundland. In the Old World they stretch from Ireland to the Bering Sea, spanning the huge landmass of Europe and Asia. In the north of America on Ellesmere Island at 76° N, red foxes are well within the Arctic Circle. In the south they are almost within sight of the Tropics when they reach the coast of Texas (30° N). Between these extremes they are found coast to coast, with the exception of Arizona, southern Florida and a sliver of land running north-south from Alberta in Canada to Mexico. The red fox that haunts the copse and pasture of a traditional English landscape is just as much at home in the deserts of the Middle East or Spanish Sahara with scarcely 3 in (8 cm) of annual rainfall, or in Arctic tundra (where they only begin to shiver at 9°F (−13°C), on Alpine passes at over 13,120 ft (4000 m), or in the concrete jungles of central London.

In competition between canids that are very similar, the general rule is that larger dog species dominate, or even kill, smaller ones. Gray wolves chase and kill coyotes, coyotes kill kit and swift foxes, golden jackals kill red foxes, and red foxes kill Arctic foxes and gray foxes. However, in some areas smaller foxes are, paradoxically, protected by their size. This is illustrated by the distributions of the red and Arctic foxes. The range of the two species overlaps in the Eurasian and Canadian tundra. Both species are impressively adapted to the cold, and both are remarkably similar in everything they do. Red foxes, being 50 per cent heavier than Arctic foxes, treat them as smaller, and thus inferior, copies of themselves and overpower them when they meet. However, the heavier red foxes need to eat far more and towards the north food becomes too thin on the ground to sustain them. The larger body that allows the red fox to bully the Arctic fox further south gives it an appetite that cannot be satisfied in the north. So, the red fox's brute strength sets the southern limit to the Arctic fox's range, while its hefty appetite sets its own northern limit.

The balance between Arctic and red foxes is also affected by climate and is so fine that even small changes in climate, such as the warming of the northern hemisphere over the last century, can have a noticeable effect. For example, between 1880 and 1940 the mean annual temperature increased by 4.5°F (2.5°C) in Spitzbergen, bringing it a climate previously enjoyed 900 miles (1450 km) to the south. This rise led to an increase in prey that allowed red foxes to invade territory that was previously the refuge of Arctic foxes. The invading red foxes pushed Arctic foxes out of the warmer, low-lying coastal areas to high-altitude inland sanctuaries.

The white morph of the Arctic fox in Greenland, showing the gray summer pelage.

Weighing only 2 lb 3 oz–3 lb 5 oz (1–1.5 kg), the fennec lives deep in the Sahara and is the smallest of all foxes. While the Arctic fox does not shiver until temperatures plummet to −70°C (−94°F), the fennec starts to tremble with cold at less than 20°C (68°F), and neatly wraps its tail like a stole around its nose and feet. However, it has an amazing record of its own: the fennec fox only starts to pant when the temperature exceeds 35°C (95°F), and its jaws open to a full pant only at 38°C (100°F). But when it pants, it really pants, its resting rate of 23 breaths per minute rockets to a maximum of 690 breaths per minute.

The desert fennecs shelter underground during the heat of the day and hunt in the cool of dusk and dawn. They rarely drink, and obtain moisture from their food, which includes small rodents, lizards, birds and insects. These foxes are adapted to conserve as much water as possible. A panting fennec curls its tongue up, so as not to waste even one precious drop of saliva. Its butterfly-shaped ears constitute 20 per cent of its body surface and, when the temperature soars, it dilates the blood vessels in its ears and feet. This allows more hot blood to flow through its extremities, increasing the amount of heat radiated to the outside. If the air temperature climbs higher than its normal body temperature of 38.2°C (100.8°F), the fennec lets its body heat up to 40.9°C (105.6°F), thus reducing the water it has to 'waste' in sweating. The fennec also saves energy by having a metabolism that chugs along at only 67 per cent of the rate predicted for such a small animal. Similarly, its heart rate of 118 beats per minute is 40 per cent lower than expected for its body size.

In 1981 the amazing news came that a new desert fox had been discovered in Israel. It weighed only 2 lb 3 oz (1 kg) and had large ears, a stupendously fluffy tail and naked footpads. Eventually it was identified as Blanford's fox, which meant that it was not a new species but an old one in a new place. This sister species of the fennec had previously been known only from remote hills in Afghanistan and Iran, so the Israeli specimen was at least 870 miles (1400 km) out of place. Using their sinuous tails as a flamboyant counterbalance and naked pads for high-traction grip, Blanford's foxes bound with feather-light grace up near-

North American red foxes, such as this one from Utah, are instantly distinguishable from their European counterparts by their finer, longer coats.

vertical surfaces on scree, cliff and crag. Indeed, they expend far more energy during activity than other desert foxes living in flat areas. Blanford's foxes live in pairs, sharing cliff territories of 0.2–0.8 sq miles (0.5–2 sq km) as they search for beetles, grasshoppers, spiders and berries, especially relishing capers. Like the fennec, they rely on such food for moisture as well, and may increase their consumption of fruit in the hot summer, to compensate for deficiencies in water.

The ability of the Blanford's fox to live on cliffs explains how it can coexist with the fennec of shifting sands. The fennec's range also overlaps, to the south, that of the 4 lb 6 oz–7 lb 14 oz (2–3.6 kg) pale fox of the southern Sahara, and, to the north, that of the 4 lb 6 oz (2 kg) furry-footed Rüppell's fox. Compared with the tiny fennec and Blanford's, the Rüppell's is a newcomer to the desert scene, being a miniature version of the red fox from which it recently descended. In addition, red foxes also penetrate Middle Eastern deserts where they are 6 lb 9oz (3 kg) waifs compared to their European brethren, which can weigh over 22 lb (10 kg).

In these areas the small Rüppell's fox may thrive in arid landscapes too impoverished for the larger red fox. Elsewhere, competition between the two species may be defused by exaggerated differences in the lengths of blades on their lower scissor-teeth. These differ more in parts of Israel where reds and Rüppell's coexist than they do where only one of these species occurs, perhaps allowing them to specialize in different diets. It seems odd that such small adjustments in chewing teeth could allow them to cohabit. However, a similarly small distinction separates the larger canine teeth of red foxes from those of the gray foxes with which they coexist in the U.S.A.

There are also species that diverge in size in some areas, such as the Chilean or South American gray fox, *Dusicyon griseus*, and Culpaeo, *Dusicyon culpaeus*, of the Andes. These two descended from a common ancestor less than half a million years ago, and differ principally in that the Culpaeo has longer canine teeth. Northern Culpaeos and grays are both about 28 in (70 cm) long, whereas in southern Chile they are 35 in (90 cm) and 24 in (60 cm) long respectively. The northern Andes are high and the great altitudinal range of habitats provides a diversity of rodent prey, while in the lower southern Andes, prey diversity diminishes. The

Several species of wild canid may coexist –
competition diminished by differences in size.
In the Middle East, the all-purpose red fox is larger
than its scaled down miniature, the desert Ruppell's
fox (top left) while the fennec (top right) is yet
tinier. The Blanford's fox (left) lives on cliffs.

size difference between the two species in the south may be due to lack of habitat and prey diversity forcing them into competition.

The foxes provide marvelous examples of evolution in action. For example, between 10,000 and 16,000 years ago gray foxes reached islands off the shores of California. At this time a group of three northern islands were a single landmass and were probably reached by rafting or swimming foxes. The three southern islands, however, were never connected either to the northern islands or to the mainland. Gray foxes only reached the southern islands 3000 years ago. This species derived directly from the northern island populations and was most likely transported by native Americans arriving in the Californian Channel islands 9000 to 10,000 years ago. On all six islands there are miniature replicas of the gray fox found on the mainland, most of them distinguished as subspecies. Called the Island fox, *Urocyon littoralis*, they weigh between a mere 2 lb 6 oz and 6 lb (1.1 and 2.7 kg), whereas their larger Californian counterpart weighs 11 lb (5 kg). The exact reason for the size differences between the two species is unclear, as the habitat on the island is very similar to that on the mainland. The reason may be differences in diet. The Channel Island fox is primarily insectivorous, whereas the gray fox eats a wider variety of vertebrate prey found only on the mainland.

The three northern subspecies of the Island fox on the northern three islands have recently declined dramatically. Fewer than six individuals are now known on San Miguel, for example, from a population of several hundred in 1993. Golden eagle predation and disease have been implicated in the decline but the reasons are really unknown. A high-priority plan to save the species on the northern islands, including captive breeding, has been initiated by the National Park Service.

However, less than 125 miles (200 km) to the south, on San Clemente island, another subspecies of the Island fox (found only on San Clemente island) is being killed by the U.S. Navy in an attempt to eliminate predators of the San Clemente island shrike, itself an endangered subspecies of the widely distributed loggerhead shrike. This story is paralleled by that of the endangered Asiatic wild dog or dhole (locally known as the ajag). A Javanese

The gray zorro is one of the small South American canids.

subspecies of the ajag hunts banteng, a wild cow, which is also endangered. Both situations present dreadful dilemmas for conservationists.

The 12 lb (5.4 kg) South American canid, the Amazonian crab-eater, *Cerdocyon thous*, is one of the eight South American zorros. Despite their name, Amazonian crab-eaters almost never eat crabs. They are omnivorous, fruit being their most frequent food. These zorros look remarkably similar to side-striped jackals, they show no sexual dimorphism, and live in social units of two to five adults (usually a pair and their offspring).

Another of the South American foxes is Darwin's fox, *Pseudalopex fulvipes*, also known as Chiloé fox. Previously believed to be endemic to the Chilean island of Chiloé, a small disjunct population was discovered 373 miles (600 km) away on the mainland in Nahuelbuta National Park, in the 1970s. These two populations have been separated for about 15,000 years and both are thought to be relicts of a former more widely distributed species. The future of Darwin's fox is bleak.

Despite international protection the fox is still persecuted for raiding poultry, and poached for zoos and the pet trade. The mainland population exists within an 'island' of pristine rainforest, less than 3 miles sq (8 km sq), surrounded by degraded farmlands and pulpwood plantations. Furthermore, the small number of Darwin's foxes in the park (probably fewer than 50) have to compete for scarce food resources with the larger South American gray fox and the culpeo, and may be preyed on by the large number of pumas present.

Today the pinnacle of canid success is the 13 lb (6 kg) red fox. This canid is the most widespread of all the wild Carnivores, adapting to desert, tundra, farmland and city, and prospering on foods from beetles and berries to beefburgers. The same build, and doubtless the same opportunism, that enabled the pioneering early dogs to prosper alongside fearsome cat-like sabre-tooths now enables the red fox to dodge the traffic in the busiest cities in Europe and North America.

The gray zorro is a generalist predator of the South American pampas, whose private life has been little studied.

Characteristics

Red foxes are the largest of all vulpine species with males weighing approximately 14 lb 5 oz (6.5 kg) and females 12 lb 2 oz (5.5 kg). They mate in January to February although this may be earlier in the south and later in the north. Gestation lasts 52 to 53 days and one litter, averaging four or five cubs, is born each year.

A red fox potentially has a lifespan comparable to that of a small domestic dog – up to 14 years in captivity. However, in the wild, life is somewhat more risky (due mostly to man and to rabies) and 95 per cent of red foxes die before their fourth birthday. Indeed, in many populations, only a minority of red foxes survive their first year.

Although red in name, red foxes can be far from red in color. Individuals throughout their range vary through shades of brown to yellowish-gray. In the north two other color phases exist: black and silver. Black and silver foxes have no reddish hairs: instead their guard hairs are black or black with a band of white. The presence of the white band results in the silvering effect and may extend over part or all of the body. Silver red foxes and red red foxes are the same species and may even be littermates. In the early nineteenth century, 16 to 25 per cent of red fox skins traded at the Hudson's Bay Trading Company in Canada were silver. Yet over 100 years this proportion fell to between 5 and 7 per cent and continues to decline. Whatever advantages the silver fox had two centuries ago do not appear to hold up in modern society.

Arctic foxes also exist in two color morphs (blue and white), and both change color from winter to summer. The white, or polar, fox is white in winter, and brownish-gray in summer. The blue fox is light brown, with a bluish sheen in winter, molting to chocolate brown in summer. Over the vast expanse of the Arctic fox's continental range, the white form predominates and less than one in a hundred is blue. On shores where snow does not settle, a white fox sticks out while a beachcombing bluish-brown fox blends discreetly with its surroundings. Not surprisingly, therefore, blue foxes are most common on smaller islands, which have a higher ratio of coastline to interior. For example, on the large island of Greenland the two colors are equally represented,

Red foxes come in different color morphs: this cub is a silver red fox.

whereas on the smaller Iceland, two-thirds of the population are blue. Blues are in the great majority along the coastline of Iceland, where white foxes are always at a disadvantage and only continue to crop up due to immigration from the interior. Inland, blue foxes are better off than whites during summer, being less conspicuous to fox-hunters, whereas white foxes are better off in winter; resulting in a mixture of both. One might expect color prejudice among Arctic foxes, with mates selected to produce young of the appropriate color for local conditions, but where they have been studied, Icelandic foxes pair up regardless of color.

All members of the dog family tend to be highly adaptable opportunists living in complex and flexible societies. The red fox is no exception. Although foxes do not come together to call in chorus as jackals, coyotes and gray wolves do, fox families keep in contact with barks and wails, and several individual voices may be heard replying to each other. Red foxes produce a wide array of different sounds that grade into one another and span five octaves, and all individuals have characteristically different voices. These sounds may be categorized as belonging to two distinct groups – 'contact' calls and 'interaction' calls. The most familiar fox sound is the 'wow wow wow' call – a sort of bark involving three to five syllables. Protracted 'wow wow wow' 'conversations' often ricochet back and forth between two or more widely spaced foxes. The call becomes quieter as individuals draw closer together and cubs are greeted by adults with the quietest version. This is similar to humans shouting 'hello' when lost in the woods, and muttering the same greeting as a preamble to shaking hands. 'Interaction' calls are heard when foxes meet at close quarters. During an aggressive encounter, foxes make a stuttering, throaty noise (sometimes termed 'gekkering') that sounds rather like a football fan's rattle, or a stick being dragged along a picket fence. Gekkering is most frequently heard during the courting season or when cubs are at play.

A call which fits into neither of these categories is the long-drawn-out monosyllabic wail ('waaaaah' – the 'vixen's scream'). This eerie and magnificent sound is most common during the breeding season and may be the call of a vixen in heat summoning dog foxes. Contrary to popular belief the call is also made by dog foxes. Another monosyllabic call is the alarm bark – generally given by an adult of either sex to warn its cubs of danger. At close quarters this resembles a muffled cough but at longer range sounds more like a sharp bark. Cubs respond to the alarm bark by diving for cover.

An Arctic fox, camouflaged on ice in Greenland.

Foxes also convey a great deal of information to one another by subtle body movements, accentuated by their body markings (the conspicuous white tag at the end of the red fox's tail and the cream fur trimming the inner edge of the black-backed ears). Thus, where a human may raise an eyebrow, grin or grimace, movements of a fox's ears, tail and mouth are laden with meaning, as is its body posture. A playful fox will have ears perked and may rear on its hind legs. A fearful and submissive fox grins in submission, its back arched and body curved, legs bent in a crouching position. Its tail beats back and forth and its ears are flush against its skull and pointing backwards. A confident fox in an aggressive attack will, conversely, have ears rotated and flattened to the side, but not backwards, and the tail will be held aloft.

Scent also plays an essential part in communication between foxes. The smell that most people associate with foxes is that of urine, but there are at least five other specific fox odors. The deposit of urine may signal occupancy of a territory but urine is also used within the territory to mark, for example, emptied cache sites. The tail gland (often called the violet gland as the fragrance is reminiscent of these flowers) is visible as an ellipse of dark guard hairs on the top surface of the tail, about 2¾ in (7 cm) from the root. Beneath these guard hairs is a patch of glandular skin 1 in (2.5 cm) long by ½ in (1 cm) wide, covered with sparse yellowish bristles smeared with sebum. The function of the gland is unknown, although it is more active during the breeding season and the odor would undoubtedly be wafted around as the tail is arched and lashed during many social encounters. A pair of bulb-like anal sacs are also at the fox's rear end, opening through 1⁄12 in (2 mm) diameter ducts clearly visible on either side of the anus. Each sac has a capacity of 0.5 cc and contains an acrid-smelling, milky fluid. Anal sac secretions are sometimes dripped onto droppings (another source of fox odor) and may be squirted out when the fox is frightened and during territorial disputes. Another set of glands, of which we also know little, is located in the skin around the chin and angle of the jaw. Foot glands produce a pleasant, sweet smell from the pinkish skin between their toes and pads – this is the scent followed by hounds, although absolutely nothing is known of its function in fox society.

Red foxes, such as this one on Round Island, Alaska, can tolerate cold almost as well as Arctic foxes.

The Search for Food

Wherever they occur, foxes (apart from the primarily termite-eating bat-eared fox) will eat almost anything they can find. They are such opportunistic hunters and scavengers, that their diet can vary greatly from one area to another, even within a species. Foxes everywhere take mammals (especially voles, lemmings, mice and rabbits) wherever the opportunity arises, and even a prickly hedgehog is neatly peeled and nibbled clean. Fruit is a universal favorite.

Despite their opportunistic natures foxes do have their specialities. The red fox is a specialist mouser. Adapting to this trade has given it a lot in common with small cats, including the ability to pounce on prey with great precision. The fox detects its prey by pinpointing the sounds of its hidden victim. The red fox can locate sounds to within one degree, and its hearing is especially acute at the low frequencies at which rodents rustle in the vegetation (3.5 KHz). Then it springs, sailing high above the quarry, beating its tail to steer in mid-air, before plummeting down to land up to 16 ft (5 m) away, and smack on target.

A number of factors help the red foxes achieve their accurate pounce. First, they normally take off at an angle of about 40°, which is close to the theoretical optimum of 45° for maximum distance. They aim lower for short jumps, and much higher, up to 80°, if they need to land with extra force, for example to break through a crust of snow. Second, red foxes have relatively longer hind legs than do other members of the dog family, and this increases their propulsive force. Third, they are much lighter than other dogs of the same size, being half the weight of a domestic dog or small female coyotes of fox length. Their skeleton is streamlined, the leg bones, for example, are disproportionately slender and weigh 30 per cent less per unit area of bone than expected.

Despite all these adaptations, there are areas where red foxes rarely eat mice, and everywhere they retain the opportunism that secured their ancestors' success. For example, in close-cropped pasture they take advantage of the easy access to succulent, crawling fare. There is great precision in a red fox's pursuit of earthworms which, as every fisherman knows, crawl to the surface on still, warm nights. The fox listens, with head cocked and ears perked, for tell-

A British red fox by night.

tale sounds over the din of rustling leaves. Suddenly, the fox freezes, brush poker-stiff and ears flicking. A worm has incautiously rasped its chaetae on the grass and the fox's snout points at the noisy indiscretion. It plunges down into the grass and the worm's head is neatly clamped between the fox's incisors, its tail wedged 'safe' in the soil. The fox avoids snapping its victim by holding the worm momentarily taut and then raising its muzzle in an arc, slowly at first, to draw the worm intact from its sanctuary. Flinging itself into contortions, the earthworm winds around the fox's muzzle, but the captor, its jaws maneuvering dexterously, slips the animated spaghetti down its throat. With a daily requirement of about 600 calories and with a worm being worth only two and a half calories, a fox would need to eat 240 earthworms each night to satisfy its energy requirements. A skilled fox can catch a maximum of four worms per minute and thus, under ideal circumstances, can make its living in an hour of leisurely strolling.

A more challenging proposition for dinner is a rabbit, a common meal for woodland foxes in southern England. Red foxes use several methods to hunt rabbits. Where there is sufficient camouflage a fox may attempt a stealthy approach, pacing slowly, half crouching, from one tree or bush to the next, until close enough to charge at top speed. Another method is to lie in wait beside a warren, just as a cat might do, to pounce on an unwary rabbit as it emerges. Even underground, rabbits are not totally secure, for foxes will dig out the shallow breeding stops on the periphery of the main warren where low-ranking, doe rabbits stow their litters. Lastly, there is the dash and grab, to which the preamble varies from a sauntering pretence at disinterest to a full-throttled charge. At the nonchalant end of this spectrum, the fox trots through a group of rabbits, seemingly oblivious of the succulent predatory temptations to left and right; something in the vulpine demeanor must reassure the rabbits which continue to graze with no more than a cautionary thump of a foot as the fox passes. Occasionally, however, the fox's disinterest is a sham, and an engrossed, nonchalant rabbit fails to notice the slight tensing in that jaunty gait that heralds a deadly swerving sprint.

Foxes are obsessive hoarders. An infant fox, of only one month old, has the well-developed instinct, not only to defend fiercely a meal, but also to make caches compulsively. Caches are

An Arctic fox pouncing on a lemming beneath the snow.

regularly moved, presumably to increase security, and are easily relocated with remarkable accuracy (it appears that red foxes memorize the exact location of their caches). With their keen sense of smell foxes are capable of discovering caches made by others. Nonetheless, it seems very much easier for a red fox to find its own caches than it is for another fox to find them. Thus, caches represent a private insurance policy against an unpredictable future. Preferred foods are hidden more often, yet how much and what is hoarded does vary and will increase in times of need (for example, before the birth of a litter) and when competition for food is high (when there are several adults in the vicinity). In Turkey, red foxes cache turtle eggs, carrying up to five in their mouth at one time to bury in the sand. Blanford's foxes are unusual in rarely or never hoarding food. Living in the desert they feed on small, perishable, water-rich foods (mainly insects and plants) which may not be worth hoarding.

Some foxes become resident in an area and establish a stable home range that they defend against neighbors and intruders (a territory). Others are itinerant and of no fixed abode. The sizes of fox territories vary greatly between areas. Red foxes living in the south of England, in farmland, woodland and in the cities generally have small territories, averaging less than 247 acres (100 ha) and maybe as small as an extreme of 25 acres (10 ha) where they use a mixture of large gardens and farmland. An urban fox in Oxford or Bristol could probably run the width of its home range in less than a minute, and yet might spend several years within its confines. The situation is markedly different in the fells of Cumbria, where home ranges average more than 2470 acres (1000 ha) and in the deserts of Oman a red fox may roam over an area as large as 12,350 acres (5000 ha). North American red foxes, similarly, can have large ranges: in Iowa and Minnesota ranges average between 1729 and 2370 acres (700 and 960 ha). In the barren grain fields of North Dakota ranges are even larger (up to 4940 acres, 2000 ha) and in the Arctic red foxes range over 8398 acres (3400 ha). The size of these territories is largely dependent on the availability of food, but they must also be defendable. The cost of defending a territory is likely to be higher for large territories and where foxes are abundant, because the territory will be bombarded by more intruders. All else being equal, territories will be smaller where food

Red fox cub with vole.

availability is greater. A territory must, however, be large enough to guarantee an adequate food source every night and must have sufficient options to cope with the worst conditions.

A territory may be shared by two or even more adult foxes. This does not necessarily incur any extra energy cost or require any enlargement of the borders but may be explained by the way in which the food supply is dispersed. In some habitats the patchiness of the food supply means that the smallest territory required to provide sufficient food for a pair will also provide a surplus to support additional group members. To ensure that they have an adequate chance of eating every night, and from season to season, a pair's territory might have to include a pasture, a warren, an orchard and a garbage tip and these may yield sufficient worms, rabbits, apples and offal to support additional group members at minimal cost to the pair. This is one example of circumstances in which the pattern of food availability may create an opportunity for groups to form. The principle may be illustrated as a game of dice, in which one die represents a food patch, and one throw determines the food availability for one night. Imagine the animal can only eat if we throw a '6' and that throwing a '6' secures only enough food for one individual for that night. Having six sides, one die gives a 1 in 6 or 16.7 per cent chance of eating. It would be imprudent to gamble an essential meal on such low odds. Given the choice, you might refrain from joining the game unless you had, say, at least an 80 per cent security of eating each night, that is an 80 per cent chance of throwing a '6'. Each 6-sided die carries a five-sixths chance of failure, thus nine dice are needed for 80 per cent food security $((1-(\frac{5}{6})^9) = 0.806)$. The principle behind this is that having secured the nine dice needed to eat at all on 80 per cent of nights, on many nights extra '6's will be available, and during those periods the territory can be shared at no extra cost.

Red foxes living on the outskirts of Oxford live in groups of four or five adults. They feed mainly on food scavenged from bird-tables and compost heaps, on windfall fruit, and earthworms. These foods are quite plentiful but also extremely variable in their availability. Whether a field is heaving with earthworms or yields none at all will change from night to night, or even hour to hour. A change in the wind will drive the worms underground before their moist bodies become chilled. So, a pair of red foxes needs several pastures to ensure that one will be in the lee of the breeze. Yet each pasture will probably provide enough worms to go

Small canids often scavenge by trailing large carnivores.

around several foxes. Similarly, households differ in when they produce scraps: in one garden foxes might find a bonanza of chicken bones one night, and nothing the next. So each territory has to encompass enough homes to give the foxes an acceptable chance of eating every night.

The same principle can be observed in other fox species. Thus, the shortest stretch of coastline productive enough to guarantee an adequate food supply for a pair of Arctic foxes will often provide enough food for a companion too. Any dead seals, or even seabirds, washed up, would be a feast for several foxes and, at other times, the junior member might have to make do with seaweed maggots (the Arctic fox's equivalent to the red fox's earthworms). This is quite different to the Arctic foxes on Wrangel Island. They live on lemmings which are uniformly spread across the tundra, so a pair of foxes can expand or contract its territory as lemming numbers soar or crash.

Although superficially very dissimilar, Blanford's foxes preying on crickets in a sunbaked canyon have much in common with Arctic foxes collecting flotsam on an icy beach. Blanford's foxes concentrate most of their hunting in the fertile floors of deeply cut wadis, rich in insect prey, within their cliff-face territories. Each territory, whatever its area, contains roughly the same amount of creekbed. The wadi of the Blanford's fox is, in effect, the productive cove of the Arctic fox. However, Blanford's foxes most often live in pairs.

The bat-eared fox of the African grasslands is a little unusual among foxes, eating primarily termites. The need to snap up termites at top speed has led to the evolution of a unique flange on the bat-ear's lower jaw. The muscle rooted to that flange enables it to mince termites at more than three chews per second. They also have extra molar teeth to grind up insects. Since termites forage in huge numbers and vanish faster than they can be eaten, the bat-eared fox loses nothing by sharing the spoils. So, families of two or three adults with attendant cubs often forage together and when one hits the jackpot, its companions will run over to join in the brief, but succulent, feast.

Whether foxes form groups where conditions allow depends on the balance of costs and benefits to each individual involved. This balance would be affected if additional group members behaved co-operatively – and sometimes they do.

Bat-eared foxes specialize in eating termites.

Sociality

Red fox groups almost always contain only one adult male. These foxes seldom travel together, and never operate as a pack, but they do meet fleetingly during their wanderings, and scent and sound keep them in contact even when they are far apart. Not all foxes live in groups but where groups do form, a social hierarchy among the members is established.

Fox groups are normally families of one dog fox and several, related, vixens. Additional vixens in a group co-operate, to varying extents, in defense of the territory and in rearing the dominant female's cubs. In fact, care of the young is one co-operative trait that, above all others, seems to unite the dog family. Associated with this trait is family planning. Among group-living dogs, whether they be wolves, jackals or foxes, the general rule is that only one female breeds. The behavior is so prevalent that it probably stretches back well before the split between wolf-like and fox-like dogs. The breeding matriarch is usually the oldest female in the group, and often the mother of her entourage of helpers. Among subordinate non-breeding vixens some individuals are assiduous helpers, playing with and grooming the cubs, guarding them and feeding them.

Red fox vixens are capable of conceiving at least 14 cubs in one litter, but in many areas the average litter size at birth is between four and five. The known extremes are averages of three in Jämtland, Sweden, and eight in southern Ontario, Canada. In some regions the average varies not only from place to place, but also from year to year (e.g. from three to six in northern Sweden). Large litters are typical where mortality is high, in which case, high productivity may compensate for high mortality. The proportion of breeding and non-breeding vixens also varies regionally. In areas where fox mortality is high, either due to fox trapping for fur or where there is a high incidence of rabies, at least 90 per cent of vixens become pregnant each breeding season. In contrast, in some urban areas of England, up to 60 per cent of females may not rear cubs.

The more rigid the hierarchy in a group, the easier it is for the dominant to manipulate the breeding of her subordinates. For example, in an Oxford suburb where red foxes lived to five

A red fox vixen nursing well-grown cubs.

years or more, generally only one vixen bred in each group. A stone's throw away, in Oxford city, although food was abundant, road traffic accidents limited the average lifespan to 18 months, and most vixens had cubs. Perhaps the hierarchy based on age that operated in the suburbs had broken down among the youthful city vixens, most of which were contemporaries.

Of course, 'birth control' in subordinate foxes is not a matter of conscious thought or decision by these vixens, and is probably not even voluntary. Rather, there is a social mechanism that determines whether or not a vixen breeds. This has the effect of concentrating the available resources for the well-being of a select few offspring. The mechanism of reproductive suppression among foxes is unknown but there are several possibilities. Vixens may fail to ovulate, they may fail to mate or conceive, they may abort or resorb their embryos, or they may fail to rear their cubs. All these phenomena happen, but the crucial mechanism remains a mystery. One possibility is that dominant vixens actively obstruct the male's access to subordinates. Almost all wild vixens do come into breeding condition, so the effect of subordination may be to switch off the scent signals that would normally advertise their receptivity, rather than switching off the reproductive system itself. Of course, the subordinate vixen may be the dog fox's daughter, so avoidance of inbreeding may explain their restraint. However, there are cases of incest in foxes and brother and sister have successfully reared cubs. Whatever the mechanism of suppression, it is likely to vary with circumstances, and may in some cases not be exerted at all. Sometimes two females will breed and may even cohabit in the same den, nursing their cubs communally. This has been seen in gray and Ethiopian wolves, golden jackals, red foxes and Bengal foxes. However, as observed in species from wild dogs to dingoes, such dual births can result in the dominant mother killing the subordinate's cubs, whereupon the bereaved mother becomes a wet-nurse for the dominant's cubs.

Whether to stay at home as a helper or set forth on a perilous journey to seek its own territory is a difficult choice for a newly adult member of a family group. If the chances of a young vixen surviving as an emigrant, or of winning a breeding territory, are very low, but her chances of inheriting her mother's territory quite high, then it might be to her advantage to stay at home even if that means postponing her own reproduction. In contrast, if her chances of securing a territory of her own elsewhere are high, then such a postponement would be

A red fox cub making its first appearance from the den.

disadvantageous. Among black-backed jackals, bat-eared and crab-eating foxes and coyotes, some individuals have left home for months on end only to return to their parental home as assiduous helpers, having presumably tested the property market and found it hostile.

Dispersal is in full swing from September until February, but may begin as early as July (the departure date varies even between littermates). Some young red foxes leave home suddenly, others initially make a succession of excursions, some oscillate between two home ranges before finally shifting their base. Some foxes weave an erratic course across the countryside, others travel fast and far in a roughly straight line. The distances over which red foxes disperse vary greatly. The record is a straight-line distance of 310 miles (500 km) recorded in Sweden. In the U.S.A. the longest point-to-point dispersal was recorded for a dog fox that covered 244 miles (393 km) (in Britain the longest is 32 miles, 52 km, in Wales). In general, dispersal distances are shorter where territories are small or where mortality is great. For instance, the ranges of resident foxes in Bristol City, Dutch farmland, Welsh hills and the American grain belt were, respectively, 111, 294, 1590 and 2371 acres (45, 119, 643 and 960 ha) while the average bee-line dispersal distances for dog foxes in these areas were 1.9, 5, 8.7 and 19.2 miles (3, 8, 14 and 31 km). Overall, the average dog fox disperses over a straight line distance roughly equivalent to the widths of four to six territories. In Ontario, where mortality was high due to rabies and fur trapping, the average dispersal distance was only 2.4 territory widths. In the Swedish taiga, foxes traveling north into relatively barren forest went further (average 18.6 miles, 30 km) than their siblings, who chose to venture south into richer lands (average 10.5 miles, 17 km). Besides securing a new territory for itself, another function of dispersal may be to avoid inbreeding. Dog foxes generally do disperse further than vixens. In the Welsh hills the bee-line dispersal distance of dog foxes was 8.5 miles (13.7 km), whereas that of vixens was 1.4 miles (2.3 km). On farmland in West Wales the figures were 2.9 and 1.2 miles (4.7 and 1.9 km).

From an evolutionary point of view, individuals have a vested interest not just in the survival of their own offspring, but also in that of other blood relatives. An individual has half its genes represented in its offspring (the other half coming from the other parent) and, half on

An Arctic fox cub in Sweden, where they are now perilously rare.

average, in its full siblings. So, by acting as a nanny, a non-breeding vixen can improve the survival of her kin, thereby promoting the survival of her own genes – a sort of breeding by proxy. Indeed if, as a result of her help, the survival of her younger sisters is doubled, then the outcome would, on average, be the same as if she had bred. In a crisis situation, when the dominant female nursing cubs dies, subordinates may adopt and successfully rear the orphaned cubs. In captivity, cubs have been adopted by two older sisters while their mother was completely incapacitated, having suffered severe injuries after a fight. The two sisters appeared to divide the duties between them, placing half the cubs in one den with one older sister, half with another.

Fathers, too, seek to maximize their surviving offspring, and among dogs, males contribute by tending pups diligently. This seems a marked contrast to most cat fathers. Two explanations commonly given for monogamy are that male assistance is necessary to rear the young or that males cannot monopolize more than one female. However, neither of these seems to be any more applicable to dogs than to most cats. A more obvious difference is that most canids eat a varied, omnivorous diet, including fruit, insects and carrion, in addition to small vertebrates. A pair eating these foods will not necessarily interfere with each other and may even feed side by side, which may encourage cohabitation in a territory and a closer link between father and pups. Although it is not common, two males do occasionally share a territory and have even been known to hunt for worms side by side without any sign of animosity.

What and where a fox can eat is also determined by social status. The most dominant members of the group generally maintain priority access to the richest pickings and spend time where choices are plentiful – for example, in gardens where scraps, fruit and worms are all abundant. In contrast, a subordinate red fox may be relegated to a field where, although worms may be bountiful, they are the only choice on the menu and may not be so bountiful when conditions are not right.

Dominance brings with it responsibility for defense. Foxes will chase intruders from their territory and will not hesitate to engage in a physical brawl, in which both participants risk serious physical injuries. Males and females are equally involved in territorial disputes. As there

A red fox cub approaching leggy adolescence.

55

are more females in the group, most episodes of territorial aggression tend to be between vixens. Relations between neighbors of the opposite sex are invariably hostile, yet between the sexes there appears to be considerable ambivalence. Although dog foxes will, and frequently do, attack females of a rival group, there are also instances when males are extraordinarily tolerant of neighboring vixens. The dominant vixens within a group tend to be those most involved in territorial defense, and even among the dominant females their response to intruders may differ depending on their position in the hierarchy. The most dominant female may be most concerned with defense of the territory. The number two ranking female may be concerned only with defense of feeding sites within the territory. The outcome of encounters between groups is also dependent on social status within the group. If, for instance, a subordinate vixen encounters a trespassing dominant neighbor, she is likely to submit despite being on her home ground. Lower-status group members tend to keep a low profile in most inter-group conflicts. These individuals may, however, be useful reserve foxes, if combined forces are needed to pursue an intruder: up to four members of a group may participate in chasing a single intruder from their territory.

The Medyni Arctic foxes, *Alopex lagopus semenovi* (a subspecies of the Arctic fox confined to Medyni Island, part of the Commander Island chain in the Bering Sea) is intriguing in its social behavior. The Medyni fox can live at unusually high densities (formerly at 1000 to 2000 animals within the coastal area of an island only 71.8 sq miles, 186 sq km) and are, therefore, in almost continuous social contact with other foxes, or their own group as well as others. Within a group, some females breed and some of the non-breeders (but not all) help at the den. Each of the groups seems to specialize on different food resources; some will feed on fish, some on seabird colonies, some at fur-seal rookeries and yet others specialize on shoreline invertebrates, such as sea urchins. Intriguingly, following a severe decline in numbers (to approximately 90 animals in 1994) due to an outbreak of mange, the foxes continued to live in groups, in which there were several non-breeders, despite the availability of substantial food resources in vacant adjoining territories.

A red fox in the Canadian Arctic.

Foxes and Humans

Men have killed foxes since time immemorial. As long ago as 2000 BC, Alexander the Great mounted on horseback, and led his Medes and Persians in pursuit of foxes, and doubtless he was not the first to hunt them. There are, and probably always have been, three views of the fox which motivate hunts: first, the fox is perceived as vermin (a predator of stock or game, or a health hazard) and killed in an attempt to limit depredations, or at least to avenge them. In the second and third views the fox is regarded as a resource, as either a quarry or a furbearer, producing either recreation or a valuable pelt.

The hunting of foxes, as both quarry and furbearer, has had a remarkable influence on human history. Trade in furs in general, and foxes in particular, largely determined the European settlement of Canada and Alaska. In 1670 the Hudson's Bay Company was chartered to ship furs to England. By 1760 more than 2000 fox skins were being exported annually from North America. The harvest of fox furs remains a large, and highly controlled, business in North America. In Ontario in the 1940s, between 50,000 and 60,000 foxes were trapped for their skins annually (more recently the number fell to between 12,000 and 20,000 due largely to rabies). In the 1970s fox fur came back into fashion. In 1979, the Ontario Trappers' Association published record prices averaging Cdn $203 (£92) per red fox pelt, with top prices of Cdn $486 (£220). The same boom gave the lower-quality British and Irish fur pelts a significant market value – numbers traded increased 15-fold in the late 1970s, and probably peaked at between 50,000 and 100,000 pelts.

Foxes were hunted, initially, as a secondary quarry, but gradually they gained importance. In the eleventh century, in Britain, the Viking King Canute classed foxes as Beasts of the Chase, a lower category of quarry than Beasts of Venery, but nevertheless higher than 'vermin'. Increasingly foxes were hunted above ground with hounds rather than below ground with terriers. Soon fox-hunting was undertaken as a noble amusement. By the late thirteenth century, King Edward I had a royal pack of foxhounds

A red fox in Scotland: the eyes may be shut but the ears are awake!

and a fox huntsman. By the Renaissance, hunting was an indispensable part of a gentleman's attainments. The destruction of deer and deer parks during the English Civil War is said to have turned attention increasingly to fox hunting. By the mid seventeenth century Britain began to be divided into fox-hunting territories and soon fox-hunting clubs formed (the first was the Charlton Hunt Club of 1737). In the eighteenth century fox-hunting exploded in popularity. At the same time in Germany, a new variant – fox-tossing – reputedly became fashionable. Foxes were persuaded to run over narrow slings of webbing, one end of which was held by a

gentleman, the other by a lady. The 'players', as is implausibly reported, tossed the fox as it walked the tightrope – a good toss being up to 24 ft (7.3 m) high. Augustus the Strong of Saxony was an enthusiastic fox-tosser and, according to dubious historical anecdote, is reputed to have tossed to death some 687 foxes in one session. The impact of fox-hunting on the English countryside has been no less remarkable: King Henry VIII designated large areas of London as parks in order that he could hunt close to home – St James', Hyde and Regent's parks were among them. The second Duke of Bolton, in the eighteenth century, tired of the long hack via London Bridge from his London home north of the Thames to his hunting grounds in the south, led the parliamentary lobbying for the new Westminster Bridge, opened in 1750. Between 1760 and 1797 there were 1539 Enclosure Acts which took common land out of smallholdings and converted it to parks and grazing land ideal for fox-hunting. Coverts were planted to hold foxes, and between 1800 and 1850 it is said that the area of gorse in Leicestershire was doubled in an attempt to create favorable fox habitat.

Worldwide there has been a colossal expansion of the fox's natural geographic range, as

The red fox, triumphant from tundra to concrete jungle, carries into the second
millennium the banner of the world's most successful wild dog. A red fox cub at full speed (left)
– canids combine speed and endurance. A British red fox (above), firing on all senses!

foxes have been transported as far afield as Australia by British expatriates, homesick for the traditions of England. The first release of foxes in Australia was in 1845 near Melbourne, Victoria, and in less than a decade the descendants of a handful of English red foxes had colonized some 5019 sq miles (13,000 sq km) of Victoria (possibly aided by transportation in the vain hope that they would control rabbits). By 1893 they were so numerous that the first fox bounty schemes were introduced. The spread of the foxes continued throughout Australia. In 1911 they had crossed the desert to arrive in Western Australia. Here they became so prolific that between 1929 and 1960 some 893,000 descendants of the original foxes were killed. Today they occur throughout mainland Australia, except in the northerly parts of Queensland and Northern Territory. A pair of foxes imported for hunting to Tasmania by two British Army officers in 1890 were destroyed, and Tasmania remains free of foxes, as does New Zealand. In Australia the red fox has been, at least partially, held responsible for the decline of the brush-tailed rock wallaby, the crescent-tailed wallaby, and the melee fowl.

Today foxes are hunted in the general sense (with dog and gun) almost everywhere, but even the mounted 'English' style of hunting is widespread. American colonists regularly imported foxhounds, the first pack being shipped to Maryland in 1650, and now there are packs of foxhounds from Mexico to Kenya.

The debate about the merits of hunting foxes on horseback with hounds is a fierce one. Hunters argue that foxes need to be controlled, that hunting is an integral part of the rural way of life, and that it contributes significantly to the rural economy. They also believe that hunting practices are conservationally sound, and that it is anyway a humane method of control. Opponents of hunting doubt its effectiveness, and hold that the cruelty involved cannot be justified in a modern society. Mounted hunts kill approximately 0.26 foxes per sq mile (0.1 per sq km) annually, amounting to less than 10 per cent of total fox mortality. As such, the lowland mounted hunts typical of southern England cannot generally be considered as anything other than a sport. Nationally, the average pack kills between 50 and 75 foxes per year, the most successful hunts averaging total kills of between 200 and 300 per season. This adds up to some 15,000 foxes killed annually by foxhounds alone, but it is highly unlikely that this limits the fox population as a whole. Another factor in the balance is that foxes eat lots of rabbits and, in areas where these eat grain crops, foxes killing rabbits may save farmers significant sums of money. Animal suffering is difficult to measure since we cannot know what it feels like to be a fox. Of course, there are many people who would find any amount of suffering unacceptable. However, the debate about the rights and wrongs of fox-hunting tend to concentrate on all-or-nothing outcomes and this tends to produce something of a stalemate. Compromises may exist to reduce the cruelty involved in hunting. For example, it is arguable that a large proportion of the cruelty involved in hunting is caused by the use of terriers in digging out foxes. A ban on this aspect of hunting would make sense if the lowland mounted packs abandoned their claims to fox control and focused on their role as a sport.

Foxes are considered by many to be pests and the idea that foxes kill for 'fun' or 'sport', or even simple malice, is as widespread as foxes themselves. There is no doubt that a single fox may wreak havoc in a farmer's hen coop or a gamekeeper's pheasant pen, killing every poult in sight. However, foxes are not unique in killing much more than they can eat (a phenomenon known as surplus killing). It is, in fact, widespread among carnivores. Furthermore, although domestic stock are often the victims, surplus killing is natural and happens in the wild. When faced with prey that do not (or cannot) run away, the fox's natural instinct to grab an opportunity to snatch additional prey may take over. This is somewhat akin to the modern man's tendency to take too much sugar! Whether or not a fox takes pleasure in killing is, of course, unanswerable.

The depth of feeling against foxes among farmers is perhaps greatest in sheep country. It has been known for one farm to lose 40 lambs to foxes in a single year and there is no doubt that losses of this magnitude amount to financial catastrophe. However, in many areas foxes rarely, or never, kill lambs. Even where lamb losses are high, and where people jump to the conclusion that foxes are to blame, starvation is probably often the true cause. A bigger puzzle may be why foxes do not kill more lambs. Indeed, foxes may dodge among lambs in pursuit of rabbits, almost as if they do not realize the lambs are food. Lamb carcasses are often left uneaten, and even where foxes do scavenge, less than a square meal is taken. Yet foxes everywhere seem to relish both sheep afterbirths and, especially, the withered tails and testes

Even in mid-winter the British red fox never grows the fulsome flame pelt of its North American cousin.

that drop off 'banded' lambs. Where foxes do prey on lambs, there is probably a tendency for them to select 'sickly' lambs, that would likely perish anyway, but this is not without exception.

In urban areas foxes are, in contrast, only occasionally considered to be a nuisance and only to a small proportion of townspeople. During the 1980s approximately one in 100 households in Oxford experienced some nuisance (at some time) attributable to foxes. Complaints ranged from predation of livestock (chickens, pet rabbits and guinea pigs) kept in their gardens, concern that foxes kill cats (most do not), dustbin raiding, scratches in the lawn, setting off security alarms on industrial premises, causing the dog to bark, taking eggs from the doorstep, entering the lounge to steal fruit from the table, pulling down the washing line and scattering lawn mowings. In general, most urban fox 'problems' are more imaginary than real and do not seem to merit widespread action. Livestock can be made inaccessible to foxes and foxes do not usually kill cats, certainly for an urban cat, the risk of being killed on the road is far greater. Nonetheless 61 per cent of townspeople questioned in Oxford during the early 1980s thought that urban foxes should be controlled (47 per cent thought that rural foxes should be controlled).

The problem of rabies in foxes is a more serious one. Rabies is a dreadful and incurable disease in man. It is invariably fatal and kills some 15,000 people annually worldwide. Only a few countries, mostly islands, are free of rabies – notably Britain, Scandinavia, Australia, New Zealand and Japan. Rabies is a more serious threat to people in undeveloped countries but can, and does, occur in developed countries; it is very expensive in both. Since the beginning of recorded history, people have dreaded hydrophobia, that awful symptom whereby rabid patients have agonizing spasms and are terrified even at the sight of water. Rabies is a viral disease of the nervous system that affects all mammals, but foxes (burdened as both the victim and the vector of this disease) are especially susceptible (foxes can contract rabies at one ten-thousandth the dose of virus generally required to infect humans) and are the principal vectors of the disease in the Northern Hemisphere. Rabies is generally spread in saliva (occasionally in urine or tissue), injected into its host when the fox is bitten by an infected animal. A rabid fox is infectious for up to six days (there are no visible symptoms at this stage), during which time the virus exists in

Adaptability is the secret of vulpine success.

such concentrations that 1ml of fox saliva could theoretically infect 34 million other foxes. Fox rabies has spread across Europe at a pace of 12.4 to 49.6 miles (20 to 80 km) per year and by the 1980s was killing an estimated half a million foxes annually. In rural areas the arrival of rabies kills 60 to 80 per cent of foxes, decimating the population. Thus, after an initial peak in the number of cases, there is a silent phase of two or three years, before the number of foxes builds up again sufficiently to sustain a further outbreak. In North America the situation is more complex since several species are involved, including red foxes, gray foxes, raccoons and striped skunks.

The problem is that killing foxes is, in most situations, ineffective. The control of foxes, as a pest and as a resource together, add up to one of the largest onslaughts on any mammalian species: in one year rabies controllers in Alberta killed 50,000 red foxes, sheep-farmers and gamekeepers in Scotland killed 9000, and fur trappers in the U.S.A. killed 356,000. Yet foxes remain widespread and abundant. There are several reasons that account for the ineffectiveness of fox control. Firstly, many foxes are killed in winter, and many of them are itinerant males who are simply passing through. Secondly, killing a territorial fox puts a vacant vulpine property on the market, and it is likely, especially in winter, that this swiftly attracts a new tenant (this is known as the 'vacuum effect'). Thirdly, if the spring population is reduced, the surviving foxes, either through having a greater share of the food supply and/or through the disruption of their social system, will probably produce young at a faster rate. A further problem encountered in trying to control rabies is that killing foxes may result in survivors coming into contact more frequently (and aggressively) in the ensuing social chaos. This, subsequently, may have the effect of increasing the contact rate of the disease (the rate at which infectious animals infect more susceptible animals). Another approach is to vaccinate foxes against rabies. Oral vaccines can be administered to foxes in the wild by using loaded bait, such as chicken heads. This has been a revolutionary success, and as a result wildlife rabies has largely been eradicated in Western Europe.

Urban foxes are of most concern regarding the risk of rabies in Great Britain, which is a heavily urbanized country, with towns densely packed with people, dogs, cats and foxes: circumstances which could be uniquely disastrous in an outbreak of rabies. However, Britain is currently free of rabies and, as an island, has a good chance of remaining so if people respect the laws regarding vaccination and travel with their pets.

Fox-like Canids

The 36 species that comprise the Canidae or dog family can loosely be divided into the vulpine foxes, of which there are 14 species, and the wolf-like or lupine canids, together with a handful of species whose ancestors were distinct before the vulpine/lupine split some 6 million years ago. The so-called foxes of South America – perhaps better referred to as the zorros – fill fox-like niches but are evolutionarily closer to the lupine lineage.

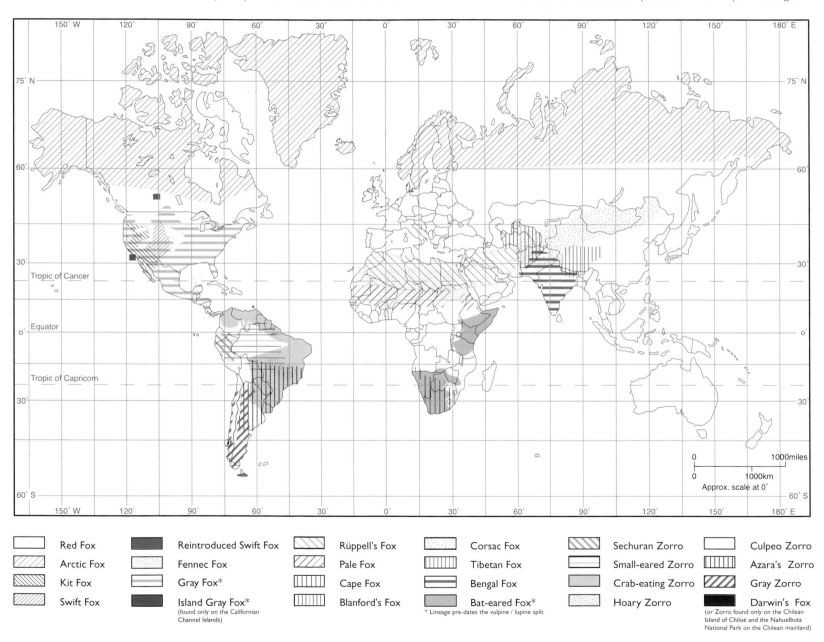

Red Fox	Reintroduced Swift Fox	Rüppell's Fox	Corsac Fox	Sechuran Zorro	Culpeo Zorro
Arctic Fox	Fennec Fox	Pale Fox	Tibetan Fox	Small-eared Zorro	Azara's Zorro
Kit Fox	Gray Fox*	Cape Fox	Bengal Fox	Crab-eating Zorro	Gray Zorro
Swift Fox	Island Gray Fox* (found only on the Californian Channel Islands)	Blanford's Fox	Bat-eared Fox* * Lineage pre-dates the vulpine / lupine split	Hoary Zorro	Darwin's Fox (or Zorro found only on the Chilean Island of Chiloé and the Nahuelbuta National Park on the Chilean mainland)